KY
KLÀ
DA

Architectures of Healing

Cure through Sleep,
Touch, and Travel

kyklàda.press

Published by kyklàda.press
an imprint of PHOTOGRAPHIC
EXPANDED PUBLISHING ATHENS

978-9-464202-85-4
D/2021/15058/06

@kyklada.press
www.kyklada.press

Asklepieia: 1
Architectures of Healing
400 BC to 200
David Bergé

The Healing Power of Sleep 9
Milica Ivić

The Healing Touch 41
Antigone Samellas

My Grandmother's 65
Desire to Heal:
A Pilgrimage to Lesbos
Valentina Karga

Asklepieia:
Architectures of Healing
400 BC to 200
David Bergé

ailing bodies and their slaves
leaving urban centers
walking for days
through mountainous fields
in pain—physical, psychosomatic,
delirious
dry grasses, rocks, trails, sea views
valleys unfolding.

walking for days
in new smells and new air
against the wind, under the sun
new scapes engage the senses differently
opening up mental space ahead of you.

walking towards
sacred healing sanctuaries
emotional tension
healing process:
hope + trust.

asklepieia
architectures conceived for divine encounters
medicine
between science and religion.

seeking divine access
not by active submission (singing, praying)
this is a pilgrimage
a distinct effort
to connect through
dreaming and awakening
away from the body
and back to the body.

healing temples
embedded in spectacular landscapes
squatting in pre-existing sanctuaries
annexes in the periphery
continually being redesigned
reformulated
confusing
future archaeologists and scholars
seeking evidence
for activity and protocols
reading epigraphic and literary sources.

dedicatory reliefs carved in marble
depicting fragile bodies surrounded by
gestures and bodies of support:
slaves, priests, to-be-offered animals,
relatives, and temple staff

serviced economies
bringing participants to sleep
snakes twirling over mosaic floors.

low benches in olive wood
density and mass of marble volumes
walls in local stone, seating integrated
geometric patterns in flooring
supportive sculptures of other goddesses
an irregularity in the masonry
—touch of life.

manipulating the course of water
through the temple:
staircase-like fountains towards
cisterns holding water
towards smaller basins
ceramic vessels and pipe systems
filling up full-body immersive baths
water for drinking.

pre-incubation rituals:
hydrotherapy
assistance in cleansing bodies
freezing water to wash off travel dust
and other external influences
patients fasting
abstaining from food and
sexual encounters
taking off
rings belts shoes.

enkoimeterion or *abaton*
incubation dormitories and
ante-chambers
for short or long-term treatment lasting months
in groups, private
in smaller temples
gender mixed—or not
sleep seekers on *klinai*, permanent beds
or *stibades*, temporary wooden daybeds
twig mattresses
animal skin on hard straw mattresses
stone for pillow
stoic floor-sleeping
physical discomfort for
a highly individualized experience
expecting the miraculous to happen
a state of receptivity
as senses evolve into dreamstate.

the moment you wake up
and your fingers have not yet
light touching the skin of your eye.

porticoed walkway
to enter temple
highest architecture of the time
ornamented with marble inscriptions
proof of previous and successful healings:
ears eyes genitalia legs and arms
to intimidate new patients
for them to tune in with

a field of expectations.

a narrow passage
into a long and wide colonnaded corridor
(leftovers from the hellenistic temple
earlier there)
harsh sun piercing through columns
—perceived space in high definition—
symmetrically structured portal architecture
in harsh contrast
with
the ill and weakened, sick and chaotic bodies
of the patients:
human definition.

white chitons uniform the sleepers
becoming temporary community
erasing cast and body differences
to sleep in incubation rooms
the *abaton*, the *enkoimeterion*
as close as possible to the heart
of the temple
mattresses aligned with altars
stones with walking history
sand and mud
wide stairs to mosaic and marble floors
rats rushing to get a share in the
to-be-sacrificed meat.

inner spaces left as vacant as possible
for the mind to engage

engage into incubation
incubation shrines:
enclosed rooms for sleeping
under the open sky
sleep in a scale different to
your bedroom's.

transformation through individual dreams
surrounded by other sleepers
direct corporal participation
an architecture to connect
through sleep
in exchange for
(animal) offers.

awakening
consultants and priests on standby
providing support in interpretation
application of dreams to the body
institute sanctions those who
neglect offering.

asklepieia
magnets for curative processes
Pergamon Piraeus Kos Athens
Oropos Corinth Lissos Lebena.

David Bergé is an artist living in Athens and Brussels. He works with site-specific interventions, installations, Walk Pieces, and book projects.

Lissos Asklepieion, Crete. Site visit, June 2021.

National Archaeological Museum, Athens. Marble reliefs. Site visit, June 2021.

Archaeological Museum of Piraeus, Piraeus. Marble reliefs. Site visit, June 2021.

Baker, Patricia. "Viewing Health: Asclepia in their Natural Settings." Religion in the Roman Empire 3, no. 2 (2017): 143–63.

Martzavou, Paraskevi. "Dream, Narrative, and the Construction of Hope in the Healing Miracles of Epidauros." In Unveiling Emotions: Sources and Methods for the Study of Emotions in the Greek World, edited by Angelos Chaniotis, 177–204. Stuttgart: Franz Steiner Verlag, 2012.

Melfi, Milena. "The Archaeology of the Asclepieum of Pergamon." In Praise of Asclepius: Aelius Aristides, Selected Prose Hymns, edited by Donald A. Russell, Michael Trapp, and Heinz-Günther Nesselrath, 89–114. Göttingen: Mohr Siebeck, 2016.

Petsalis-Diomidis, Alexia. "The Body in Space: Visual Dynamics in Graeco-Roman Healing Pilgrimage." In Patterns of Pilgrimage in Antiquity: Seeing the Gods, edited by Jaś Elsner and Ian Rutherford, 183–218. Oxford: Oxford University Press, 2005.

Renberg, Gil H. Where Dreams May Come: Incubation Sanctuaries in the Greco-Roman World. Leiden, Boston: Brill, 2017.

Riethmüller, Jürgen W. Asklepios: Heiligtümer und Kulte. Heidelberg: Verlag Archäologie und Geschichte, 2005.

von Ehrenheim, Hedvig. "Greek Incubation Rituals in Classical and Hellenistic Times." PhD diss., Stockholm University, 2011.

The Healing Power of Sleep
Milica Ivić

In most social arrangements, healing is a pause imposed by ailment, a separation from the flow of life that needs to be reconfigured. Healing is a socio-somatic process, not only a somatic state. In the traditional notion of healing, the final aim of that pause is returning to some form of 'normal social order,' to family and friends. The juxtaposition between order and disorder is inherent to the healing process. In the (post-)pandemic turmoil we live in, we can ask ourselves to which social order we return when healed. What sort of social relations is our health meant to restore to?

Sleeping is an example of a curative process that, observed in different times and social contexts, reveals a part of the complexity of the healing achieved through the acts we share with other human beings. A compelling elaboration on the social dimension of sleep can be found in Jonathan Crary's 24/7: *Late Capitalism and the Ends of Sleep*, where the author claims that "as the most private, most vulnerable state common to all, sleep is crucially dependent on society in order to be sustained."[1] Sleeping is a vulnerable state for an individual and it represents a pause in the homogeneity of time achieved through continuous operations of a networked, globalized world in the third decade of the 21st century.

In this text, I intend to unfold a reverie on the healing potentialities of sleep today, the social relations it questions and reveals, originating from a fascination of restorative examples from the past. With respect to the fact that healing includes an aspect of self-preservation that at the same time isolates us and connects us with others, I will present different examples of sleeping as a healing practice, to point out the relations between the self and the others, immunity and community, individual and the common. The examples chosen are different in terms of hierarchies, cultural context, and social order, and their selection responds to the initial intention to dwell on the consequences of the immunization politics, as conceptualized by the Italian theoretician Roberto Esposito. Immunity has various dimensions, politically, legally, socially, and medically, but Esposito focuses on an accelerated need for immunitarian security, which brings to light both the self-preserving aspect of immunity as well as the danger of the total rupture of the social bonds that immunisation implies.[2] The course of this fabulation may not be consistent, but the mosaic of its inputs hopefully expands the imaginative horizon on the sociality of healing practices.

Asklepieia, Incubation Temples

Therapeutic incubation (*enkoimesis*) was a multifaceted religious phenomenon in Ancient Greece and a widespread practice based upon a deliberate act of sleeping and dreaming in sanctuaries dedicated to the god Asklepios. The father of the goddess *Hygieia* (Health), Asklepios, was the only Panhellenic god who exclusively practiced medicine. He was depicted as an omnipotent god performing healing miracles, and as the medical practitioner who issued advice through prescriptions. Asklepios's attention was sought by those suffering from chronic, non-terminal ailments, mainly physical, that could not be cured by applying doctors' medical knowledge of the time, so the help from a divine physician was needed. Those included a wide range of problems that were circulating as oral tales originating at the sanctuaries: paralysis or lameness, blindness, parasites, unusual growths, unhealed sores, and infections, gout, kidney stones, embedded weapon fragments, and even baldness, infertility.

Incubation, widely used by the Ancient Greeks as a healing method, can be detected in the Near East long before Greek civilization began engaging with the practice. Long after that, other

Fig. 1

cultures and religions followed, evidenced in Roman times, Christianity, and Islam. Dreams were the most familiar territory, the most common human capacity that was available to everyone. There was and is no privileged dreaming, and unlike all other approaches to oracles exclusively reserved for royalty and high-ranking priests, the healing process through incubation was accessible for whoever brought an offer, whether this was a living animal or a votive made of expensive or cheap materials.[3]

Healing methods varied from directly treating the problem or touching the pilgrim/patient by hands (or tongue in the form of a snake); applying cures or medical substances, to even surgery.

Indirect methods included a wide range of remedies, physical regimens, special food and beverage diets, based or substances extracted from plants or animals. In the abundant circulation of oral tales originating at the sanctuaries, anecdotes show different possibilities of curing methods and the application of therapeutic dreams. A central role was given to events and encounters occurring in sleep, which became a threshold between illness and health, and the sovereign healing territory where anything was possible.

Incubation could be provided for a single individual in certain Asklepieia temples, while at others, it was possible for entire groups. In the temple complexes at which numerous worshipers would crowd into incubation dormitories seeking to be cured or given prescriptions by Asklepios, a symbolic field was formed which made it possible to explain, communicate and memorialize the experience of sickness.[4] Not rarely one of the god's instructions to visitors was to leave a record of their experiences, which explains the significant number of literary and epigraphical sources, dedicatory reliefs, testimonial inscriptions, stelas.

The surviving testimonial inscriptions, formally labeled "Healings by Apollo and Asklepios," provide the greatest amount of information about the practice of incubation in the sanctuary.

"Dating to roughly 350–300 BC, these testimonies are third-person accounts of medical miracles as well as other remarkable

Fig. 1
Asklepios touches a reclinging sick woman, supported by Hygieia at the Asklepieion of Pireaus, 350 BC. Part of votive relief for Asklepios, currently at the Archaeological Museum of Piraeus, Piraeus, 2021.

divine feats, and appear to have been collected by priests or cult officials, whose primary sources would have been dedicatory texts and oral traditions, for the primary purpose of encouraging the sick in their hope of regaining their health with the god's help, but also of warning those who would scoff at the tales of the god's miraculous achievements or might be tempted not to reward the god after regaining health."[5]

Those falling asleep together in the same place were all expecting a visit from Asklepios to get healed directly or receive instructions for healing. By collective sleeping, each patient got merged with stories and inscriptions about other people's sufferings and by exchanging experiences, expectations, and hopes. The moment of waking up was when everyone was surrounded by other people's sleeping/dreaming experiences and comparative evaluations.

Although everyone was engaging in dreams for easing their own ailment, pilgrims got immersed into sensing and imagining the sufferings of others, and there is a relation to others that is inherent to the healing process, divine and human, now, in the past and the future. While writing these lines, I came across the Nap Ministry[6] statement that "Naps are time travel. You can receive an inspiring message while resting. It's a third space that facilitates deep healing. It makes sense why the toxic systems don't want you tapping into this sacred place. This is why we resist." I perceive it as a contemporary conceptualization of healing practiced through sleep.

The Nap Ministry

This statement comes from an Instagram post published on February 13, 2021, by the Nap Ministry, a USA-based collective founded by Tricia Hersey, who is also called the "Nap Bishop." It originates from a presupposition that there have been multiple traumas caused by the systems in place, and identifies sleep deprivation as a racial and social justice issue.

Hence the possible causes of the need for healing are expanded. They can evolve from a personal corporeal ailment, psychological trauma, or unexpected crises such as epidemics, pandemics or natural disasters. The Nap Ministry proposes collective forms of self-preservation and resistance such as sleeping, resting, napping, pausing, sleeping and questions whether sleep is just a common human capacity and is it our common territory. Is sleep reserved for the privileged ones? In pandemic times, it might become more evident that tools for self-preservation, isolation, and rest are not available for everyone. Still, these times must emphasize the existing consequences of colonization, white supremacy, real and formal subsumption, the urge for productivity and actualization. When productive operations do not stop, and profit-generating networks function 24/7, sleep remains one of the rare "natural conditions" that capitalism cannot (yet) eliminate. It is no wonder that the Nap Ministry introduces sleep as the rare real-life event whose restorative inertness counters the deathliness of all the accumulation, financialization, and waste that have devastated anything once held in common.[7]

In the Nap Ministry's understanding, there is no normal social order to return to. Healing is an act against the existing order based on "laziness and idleness."[8] The Nap Ministry believes in a transformative and healing experience that rejuvenates and opens the mind to new possibilities. What they call sacred spaces for the community to nap together seem like private or public rooms big enough for temporary transformation into collective dormitories. Collective sleeping does not require a special space or time frame. It doesn't have to be a long, uninterrupted night's sleep. A nap, as a short sleep, especially during the day, emphasizes the need to use any opportunity to exclude oneself from the over accelerated rhythm of production. As a reaction to the centuries of prolonged sleep deprivation of black bodies, the Nap Ministry tends to guide intentional and slow exploration of the importance of creating a sustainable healing ritual via naps. What it suggests is "more than a nap (...). It's about community care: the idea of communal care, mutual aid, and interconnection with each other. We offer care to people who live in a place that doesn't give them that care." Healing is proposed as a collective responsibility, a community-based articulated activistic practice through sleep.

We can sleep near others, but we fall asleep alone. We dream alone, but at the same time, each dream is an actualization of the common human capacity in a unique, unprecedented way. One dream can never exhaust the potentiality of the given capacity. There is always 'more than me' in my dreams. Tricia Hersey believes that information is waiting for us in our dreams. Healers in the form of gods or ancestors are there, evoking this 'more than me' inherent to human capacities. Relying on them in a commonly produced secure environment becomes a political healing project. The Nap Ministry is not the only initiative pointing out the importance of rest-as-resistance practices, but it is vital for this divergent research because it articulates the connections between healing, sleep, and the need to expand the field of social imaginary.

Healing through Sleep as Common Good

Research claims that healing rituals in Asklepieia were a shared experience, narrated, transferred, and formed into diachronic *communitas*, imagined community of the sick. *Iamata* (inscribed records of cures performed by Asklepios) display a complex and layered relationship between texts, persons, and bodies.[9] Applying the term communitas to incubation in Ancient Greece is certainly an anachronism, but it helps us think about healing practices in the present times. Communitas is introduced into critical theory by Esposito, and is inseparable from immunitas. The terms communitas and immunitas share the same root, which Esposito finds in the Latin word *munus*, "a task, obligation, duty; also in the sense of a gift to be returned." Munus is a specific type of gift, the specificity of which denotes the exchange. When someone accepted the munus, an obligation to exchange was created either in the form of goods or services. The entire focus lies in the transit act of giving, meaning it does not in any way imply the stability of possession or the dynamics of acquisition, but the transfer, confiscation, loss.

    The original meaning of the term *communis* would be the one who has a responsibility, a task. It follows that communitas (com+munus) is the sum of persons who are not united by some possession, but necessarily by debt, not by that which is 'additional,' but by that which is deficient. Communitas is not a utopian optimistic political vision. Esposito does not idealize the community. "The immunized models of community, where members are protected against foreign substances, external threats, and internal contagions, so common in our times, are imploding at a frightening pace."[10] Immunity (in+munus) is a biological concept or a medical term and a socio-political metaphor. Defensiveness is inherent to the idea of immunity, as it should protect the body from diseases and people who carry diseases, but it also implies exceptions from service or obligation.

> "The immunity system is necessary for survival, but when it crosses a certain threshold, it starts destroying the body it aims to defend." There is no community without immunization. Mechanisms that communities use for immunization are the state, the law, etc. and Esposito warns about the consequences of these mechanisms taken too far. Western democracies are based on an immunitarian obsession with protecting individuals and their private wealth. "Immunis is he or she who has no obligations toward the other and can therefore conserve his or her own essence intact as a subject and owner of himself or herself."[11]

Nowadays, interpretations of immunity as sociopolitical metaphors are connected to the idea of an individual who has to be protected from external dangers. It seems to be in contradiction with the conceptualization of sleep as "one of the few remaining experiences where, knowingly or not, we abandon ourselves to the care of others. As solitary and private as sleep may seem, it is not yet severed from an interhuman tracery of mutual support and trust, however, damaged many of these links may be. It is also a periodic release from individuation —a nightly unraveling of the loosely woven tangle of the shallow subjectivities one inhabits and manages by day."[12]

Drifting through sleeping as a healing practice, I come to reflect on these contradictions inherent to the character of sleep. As Crary puts it, "these would be intimations of sleep as a radical interruption, as a refusal of the unsparing weight of our global present, of sleep which, at the most mundane level of everyday experience, can always rehearse the outlines of what more consequential renewals and beginnings might be."[13] The new beginnings would have to be imagined on the territories where extreme immunization is prevented by the obligation that was given to us in form of a gift and a burden, the obligation towards the communitas. I will conclude by questioning potentialities of healing related to self-preservation and/or the preservation of social bonds. The established theoretical framework of immunization will help me draw up different practices found in the human and non-human world, in the ancient and (very) contemporary times.

As shown by the Nap Ministry, sleeping can be a call to action. An extreme example of such, can be found in the "Resignation Syndrome," a coma-like state in which children of refugee families fall into a months-long sleep and eventually recover. It implies complete withdrawal performed by children who cease to walk or talk, or open their eyes, as presented in the documentary *Life Overtakes Me*, released in 2019.[14] The withdrawal usually starts when the families are faced with the threat of deportation to their home countries and a possible refusal of asylum status. The kids look peaceful even when their worried parents exercise their sleeping bodies, hoping that corporeal activities will keep their muscles active. While being artificially nourished, taken for walks, given baths and haircuts, getting dressed and undressed, they remain in a deep sleep. The abdication of reality and trauma is a way of extreme self-protection and the last possible retreat in the given circumstances. While we deal with it as individuals, the trauma is still socio-somatic.

Unlike sleeping, animal hibernation is an involuntary, biologically imposed common state with a particular corporeal outcome. It has a different logic and, recently revealed, physiologically based healing causes. For example, the arctic ground squirrels hibernate while their neurons and their connections are shrinking and their brains are repairing. Hibernating makes them exponentially generate neural links that didn't exist before hibernating. Without the intention to romanticize this example or fully understand the medical implications of the Resignation Syndrome I take it as an example of Esposito's extreme immunization, which also shows that healing is no longer achieved merely through collectivity, nor through medicine, and that it displays the fragility and complexity of contemporary society.

However, the threat of extreme immunization is not a contemporary invention but a possible outcome of any social order. The famous case of the most extravagant Asklepios's patient, Aelius Aristides, proves that. Among innumerable anonymous worshipers searching for god's assistance in matters of personal health, Aristides stands out as a privileged individual who spent almost twenty-five years interacting with Asklepios, who was appearing in his dreams in an incubation dormitory and other locations. The self-absorbed rhetorician Aristides seems to have derived some enjoyment from the painful symptoms of a recurring somatic and psychic malaise. At the age of twenty-seven he is believed to have been summoned by the god from his home in Smyrna to the Pergamon Asklepieion, after which he experienced sometimes real and sometimes apparently psychosomatic illness.[15]

The Aristides example could represent the individual's withdrawal from the existing social arrangement without any intention of ending healing and returning to life. Nevertheless, Aristides's writings *Sacred Tales* and *To the Well in the Sanctuary of Asklepios* represent the most important resources for understanding the ancient practice of incubation. At the god's prompting, Aristides wrote down his experiences for public consumption—300 000 lines of notes, a massive text from which 5 books and a fragment of a 6th survived with 130 dreams obtained through incubation. This tremendously rich source for incubation in general also proves the overcoming of extremely individual motivation for engaging in healing practice. Sharing the experience with others can make it a common good. The healing power of sleep today is to be found in optimistic projections, which predict that it is still possible to imagine a different future where healing is achieved through social acts, together with other fellow (human) beings.

Milica Ivić is an artist and art theorist from Belgrade. Her theoretical work is mainly inclined to the archiving, institutionalization, and production of contemporary dance.

1. Johnathan Crary, 24/7: Late Capitalism and the Ends of Sleep (London, New York, Verso: 2013), 24–5.

2. Roberto Esposito, "The Biopolitics of Immunity in Times of COVID-19: An Interview with Roberto Esposito," interview by Tim Christiaens and and Stijn De Cauwer, Antipode, June 16, 2020, https://antipodeonline.org/2020/06/16/interview-with-roberto-esposito, accessed in August 2021.

3. Alexia Petsalis-Diomidis, "Between the Body and the Divine: Healing Votives from Classical and Hellenistic Greece," in Ex-Voto: Votive Giving Across Cultures, ed. Ittai Weinryb (New York City: Bard Graduate Center, 2016), 49–75.

4. Calloway B. Scott, "Asklepios on the Move: Health, Healing, and Cult in Classical Greece" (PhD diss., New York University, 2018), 99.

5. Gil H. Renberg, Where Dreams May Come: Incubation Sanctuaries in the Greco-Roman World (Leiden, Boston, Brill, 2017), 172–73.

6. The Nap Ministry, Instagram account, (@thenapministry).

7. Crary, op.cit., 62, 74, 128.

8. Mikeisha Dache Vaughn, "Rest as Resistance: Why Nap Ministry and Others Want Black People to Sleep," Complex, May 20, 2021, https://www.complex.com/life/black-power-naps-rest-as-resistance, accessed in August 2021.

9. Scott, op.cit., 99.

10. Greg Bird and Jonathan Short, "Community, Immunity, and the Proper. An Introduction to the Political theory of Roberto Esposito," Angelaki. Journal of the Theoretical Humanities 18, no. 3 (2013): 1–12.

11. Roberto Esposito, Terms of the Political: Community, Immunity, Biopolitics, trans. Rhiannon Noel Welch (New York: Fordham University Press, 2012), 39.

12. Crary, op.cit., 126.

13. Crary, op.cit., 129.

14. Kristine Samuelson and John Haptas, Life Overtakes Me (Netflix, 2019), accessed in August 2021.

15. Renberg, op.cit., 201.

Fig. 2
Hygieia, the goddess of health and hygiene, bending to feed a snake. Marble sculpture from 380-370 BC, found in Epidaurus. National Archaeological Museum, Athens, 2021.

Fig. 3

Fig. 3-5
Asklepieion of Lissos, Crete, June 2021.

Fig. 5

Fig. 6
Amphiaraos curing a patient by touch. Votive relief in pentelic marble found in the sanctuary of Oropos 400-350 BC. Panel in the background refers to the sacred area in which the healing is taking place. The snake as a symbol of regeneration, today still associated with medicine.

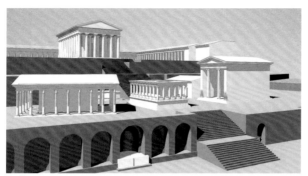
Fig. 7

Fig. 8

Fig. 7
Simulated representation of the Asklepieion of Kos,
as in 2nd-3rd century.
Fig. 8
Panoramic view of the Asklepieion of Kos, 2004.

Fig. 9

Fig. 10

Fig. 9
The Sleeping Hermaphrodite (2nd century) and Asklepios (2nd century). National Archaeological Museum, Athens, 2021.

Fig. 10
According to the inscription in the triangle part above, this votive relief in marble was dedicated to Lysimachides, holding here a model of a human leg on which a vain stands out, indicating his disease. Found near the Enneakrounos Fountain in Athens, 4th century BC. National Archaeological Museum, Athens, 2021.

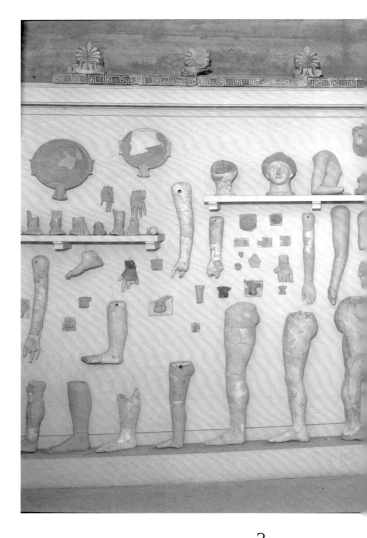

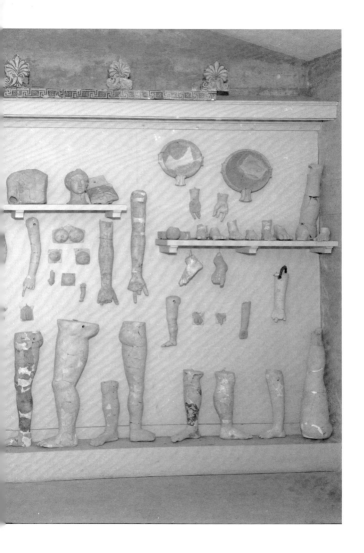

Fig. 11
Proof of healing, dedicatory reliefs found in excavations
at the sanctuary of Asklepios in Corinth, between 1929-1934.

The Asklepieion at Epidaurus was the earliest organized center for healing in ancient Greece. It shows the complexity of the cult's formation, in the same area ever since the 16th century BC, there were practices related to the securing of human health and prosperity. Initially, it was dedicated to the god Apollo with the epithet *Maleatas*, known for his healing capacities. With the continuously increasing number of worshipers, a new sanctuary, built around the middle of the 6th century BC, was dedicated to Apollo Maleatas and his son, the chthonic deity Asklepios. In the following centuries, the cult of Asklepios became predominant. Its spread in the rest of the Greek world resulted in the accumulation of great wealth in the sanctuary. The immense shrine developed in its monumental form around 390–375 BC. It included the *propylaea* (gateway), the temple built in doric style, the theater, the *odeum*, the *abaton* or *enkoimeterion* (in which patients slept on the ground), the bathhouse, the stadium, the *tholos* (rotunda, regarded as subterranean home of Asklepios), the *gymnasium* (a ceremonial banqueting hall), the *hestiatorion* (building for celebrating ritual meals), the *katagogion* (a hostel for patients and their relatives), the cistern and fountain, and several smaller sacred buildings. —*Milica Ivić*

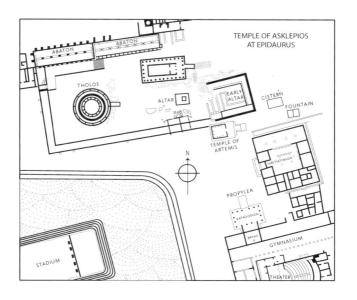

Fig. 12
The Asklepieion at Epidaurus, floor plan.

Fig. 13

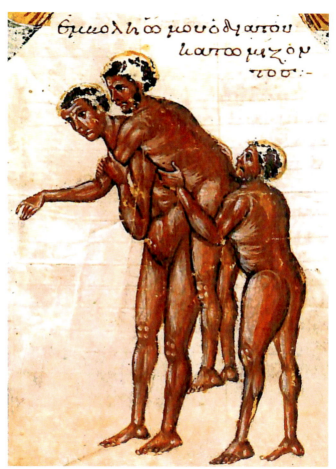

Fig. 14

Fig. 13
Pain combat in Arabic Chirurgy by means of painful application, drawing from a 10th-century surgical treatise.

Fig. 14
Putting in place a dislocated shoulder. A type of cure used for wrestlers, uplifting the patient by a person with a larger body mass. 10th-century illustration of the medical treatise by Apollonius of Citium.

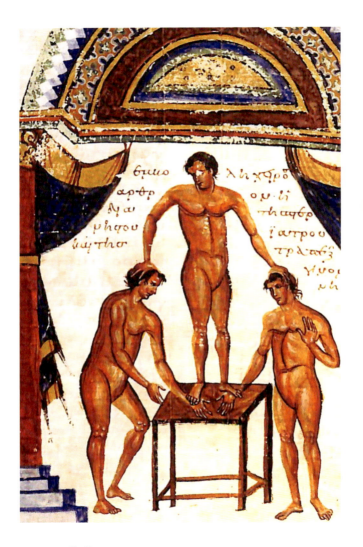

Fig. 15
A doctor using his heels to set in place the joints of the patients' hands. 10th-century illustration of the medical treatise by Apollonius of Citium.

The Healing Touch
Antigone Samellas

1. Modern Untouchability

Medical discourse and practice reflect the cultural, historically determined, orderings of the senses. Touch has been the pariah sense of modernity. At the dawn of the 20th century, bourgeois pedagogy and pediatrics frowned upon the kissing of children on the grounds that it might communicate disease. Further, behavioristic psychologists postulated that any manifestation of tenderness might foster a pathological emotional dependence of the child on its parents, thereby rendering it unfit for the world of adults. Evolutionary anthropologists assigned haptic orientation to the primitive stage of humankind, while for Freud, touch, the sense that helped infants navigate themselves through the environment, was to be superseded at a later, more mature stage by audiovisual perception. They all concurred that tactile meanderings had no place in the age of reason, an era that privileged sight and reflexivity.

The epistemological denigration of touch has encouraged desensitization, welcome at times, spear-headed by technology. In recent decades, progress in robotics has introduced the bloodless "remote control" surgery that spares the patient time and pain, though without necessarily delivering a better outcome. The healing process has almost become industrialized: healthy bodies seem to be produced automatically, like Byzantine icons 'not made by human hands.'

Touch-surrogates have prevailed upon public and private fields of sentience. In the hospitals of São Paulo, latex medical gloves filled with water when placed on the hands of the sequestered and barely conscious Covid-19 patients, produced the soothing effect of human presence and a rise in their blood flow. During the lockdown, Bluetooth-enabled "hug-shirts," and silicon lips simulated the human touch and equally elaborated earphones replicated the pulse of crowds swaying together during a rock concert. On the other hand, in contemporary art Museum Sprints—to mention the self-reflective video compilation of Florian Slotawa —have rendered the viewer oblivious of the lasting texture of the creative imprint: screen, word, and the pace of modern life leave the much-touted 'immediate experience' of art bereft of any suspicion of transcendence, thereby imbuing it with an air of prosaicness. As Claire Bishop writes: "[D]iscussions of participatory art tend to proceed with similar exclusions: without engaging with the 'aesthetic thing' in all its singularity, everything remains contained and in its place. There is merely an ethical regime of images, rather than an aesthetic regime of art."

Intimacy is also mediated by the screen, the touch screen, the touch phone. In Spike Jonze's 2013 film H*er*, a lonely writer falls in love with Samantha, a voice addressing him through the computer screen. Virtual Samantha guesses all the thoughts of her wired interlocutor and fulfills his desires. This ideal 'love affair' ruins any relationship with a flesh-and-blood woman as the 'voice' panders to the narcissistic self-sufficiency of the protagonist.

The present pandemic aggravated, absolutized, and globalized the post-modern regime of sentience, despite the very traditional and medieval character of the measures imposed: the restriction of the range of the experience of the palpable reached a climax during the successive lockdowns, when each and every one not only became untouchable to others, but also untouchable to their own self. A taboo—bare of any vestige of sacred aura—was willingly obeyed, as if we had to atone proleptically for the death we might carry inadvertently in our breath, face, and hands.

In optimistic moments, we might feel that quarantine was an exercise in tactfulness. Alphonso Lingis juxtaposes an aggressive touch that appropriates and manipulates tangible things with tact: a form of discretion that holds back one's forces and intentions to listen to what the body near us has to tell us. Tact makes the ethical stance concrete; it is a gentle form of contact that gives apt expression to respect for the other. However, untouchability as experienced during the pandemic amounted to a lowering of the eyes. Armored with a defensive evasiveness, we have been in pain out of fear; fear of contact.

According to cognitive scientists, psychological and physical pain rely on shared neural circuits: isolation, discrimination, and stigmatization give rise to 'social pain,' causing bodily distress. In contrast, holding hands with a partner, friend or relative attenuates physical pain. In general, the more extended the social connections with humans and animals are, the greater the resilience to physical malaise.

Care and healing involve palpating the suffering body with tact. Touch was fraught with danger and prohibitions even when it served as a touchstone of truth.

2. The Ambiguity of Touch

In Neoplatonic philosophy, and all its later theological elaborations, touch conveys the erotics of the intellect: the "desiring intellect," according to Plotinus, touches the divine transcendental principle the moment it ecstatically and intuitively receives its overflowing grace. Gnostic texts depict religious conversion as a *coup de foudre* that took hold of one's mind and soul, while the canonical gospels, in artistic renderings, assume that the reality of the incarnation might have been tested by the fingers of human hands. Thus, reading against the grain the Gospel of John, Caravaggio and other medieval painters have been fascinated by the episode featuring Thomas, better known as the "Doubting Thomas," who famously responded to his fellow disciples when they told him they had seen the risen Christ: "Unless I ... place my finger in the mark of the nails, and place my hand in his side, I will not believe." (*John* 20:25).

Medical practice resonated with the idea that ultimately it was neither sight nor belief, but touch that brought immediate access to the voice of nature. In the view of Christian philosopher Macrina, "the doctor who lay his fingers on the artery listened in a certain way the roar of nature articulating its proper pathology," and then interpreted the symptoms with his mind. Similarly, in the 2nd-century treatise *De Pulsibus*, Marcellinus wrote that touch "has seen even the hidden more sharply than the physician has and has often predicted what is to come," provided that long training and judgement informed the sense perception. The expansion and contraction of the arteries felt by the doctor's fingers, the sensing of the beat of the organism, spaced by pauses were tactile truths, fundamental for the prognosis and diagnosis of disease.

However, a certain maladroitness on the part of the doctor might affect the pulse of the patient, thereby marring the reliability of the diagnosis. Some physicians rushed to palpate the pulse without conversing first with the patient. Marcellinus excoriated their behavior as "indecent" and "clownish," for it alarmed the sick person thus altering his pulse. As explained by Aristotle, we shiver more when someone else touches us than when we touch ourselves. We are more sensitive to contact with another person than with ourselves. "For what is naturally connected is imperceptible. And what is hidden and sudden is more frightful to the touch."

Touch might be perceived as intrusive and humiliating. Heroes in Greek tragedy often shunned the helping hand, thinking that it would destroy them: a gesture of support was ominous of their loss of self-control and social status. Being discordant with the ancient ideal of manly autonomy, and a reminder of their vulnerability as "homo patiens," a body to lean on bespoke of their imminent emasculation. In any case, in a state of mental confusion and somatic distress the sick person appeared blinded to his own inner turmoil, and alienated from his own body. One became untouchable. Philoctetes in the homonymous tragedy of Sophocles, shied away from Neoptolemus, the son of Achilles, for he was still in pain from "the burning flux oozing from the ulcers of his louse-ridden foot." (*Phil.* 696–697, 760–767).

When we are sick, we become uncomfortably aware of the presence of our body, and particularly sensitive to the gaze and touch of others. "So unpleasant is it to everybody to have his private ills brought to light, that many have died rather than acquaint the doctors with their secret ailments." Men, according to Plutarch, were embarrassed to show a fistula of pus on their bottom, and women to expose the sore in their womb to the gaze of the doctor. (*De Cur.* 7.518d). The more secluded was the ailing subject, the greater her trepidation of the healing touch. As Marcellinus observed, "awe and fear alter the pulse of the sick when a physician who is revered and very respectable enters into the presence of children, girls or women, who were not previously accustomed to be seen in their private life, or to be repeatedly questioned about it." In today's world, feelings of shame and apprehension intermingled with fear of disease keep many women away from diagnostic centres. Women, especially those who have survived sexual abuse, feel uncomfortable about cervical screening, while, according to a recent study by Norwegian psychologists Ivanova and Kvalem, "breast cancer fear is positively associated with defensive avoidance of breast cancer screening."

"Anxiety," according to Lacan, "is precisely the feeling that arises as a result of this suspicion that comes to us of being reduced to our body." In response to this anxiety, we often evade what troubles us: we avert our gaze from our body, behaving like Mnesianax, who did not want to go out. "He said he was afraid, and if someone mentioned serious illnesses to him, he was seized by fear." (Hipp. E*pid*. 7.45). Whenever he went to the market, he saw sparks around his eyes. After he recovered and stood on his feet, he preferred to stay indoors.

Healing constituted an intersubjective process based on trust. The Hippocratic ideal, still inspiring certain strands of contemporary medicine, solicits the cooperation of the ailing person. It wants the patient to research and describe the affections afflicting him (or her). As this is not easy for the layman, the doctor has to explain to him the nature of his suffering. Then the patient manages to remember what has happened to him, and thus consents to fight the disease along with the doctor. The communication between doctor and patient made the difference between gripping and touching. In the view of Marcellinus, "experienced physicians do not seize the patient's arm with their hand as soon as they arrive, but first sit down and with a cheerful countenance ask how the patient finds himself; and if the patient has any fear, they calm him with pleasant talk, and only after that, do they move their hand to touch the patient." In all the stages of the treatment the doctor applied the requisite kind of touch.

3. The Healing Touch in the Context of a Tactile Revolution

As the Greek word for surgeon reveals, a *chirourgos* was a craftsman working with his hands. To be more precise, he could work with his feet too. In the illustration of the early-10th century Byzantine surgical manuscript, the Nicetas codex, a doctor treads with his heels on the wrists of his two patients, all of them naked but asexual, in order to put their dislocated bones in place. The doctor was a healer of ills, of bodily and mental distress. His divine-like authority resided in his ability to regenerate the ailing body and assuage the sick soul, thus bringing joy to the suffering patient. He was deemed as necessary as a builder, as charismatic and perspicacious as a prophet, and as delightful as a singer. (Homer, *Od.* 17. 384–385). Of his 'handicrafts' the healing touch spoke more than anything else of his supernatural aura and his humanitarian outlook.

In his thirteenth poem (57–62), the ancient legislator Solon admits that frequently gentle remedies could not provide relief for an ever-growing pain. Only the touch of human hands immediately restored health to the one agitated by grievous and malignant diseases.

Chronic diseases recalcitrant to the ordinary treatments and ailments that needed drastic cures vanished miraculously when the hands of the doctor or the healer god lay on the body of the sick. Votive reliefs and inscriptions depict god Asklepios

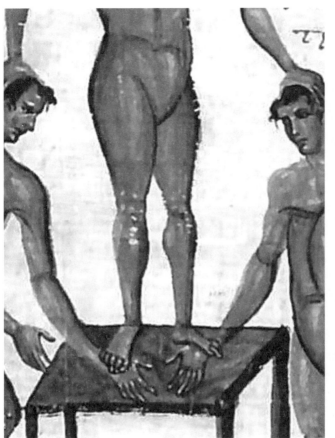

Fig. 16
Detail (Fig. 15), a 10th-century illustration of the medical treatise by Apollonius of Citium, depicting a doctor using his heels to set in place the joints of the patients' hands.

Fig. 17
Detail (Fig. 13), a drawing from a 10th-century surgical treatise, depicting a pain combat in Arabic Chirurgy by means of painful application.

Fig. 17

touching—gently or violently—the patient in order to cure him. Divinities were cognizant of the medical practices of their times. In a Hellenistic relief found in his shrine in Oropos, the healer hero Amphiaraos appears like an ordinary doctor treating with a scalpel the right shoulder of the young man Archinos. Solicitousness and attentiveness to the individual context of every disease was not divorced from scientific knowledge.

The physician, like a friend, felt obliged to stand by the one who "moved this way or that, crawling like a child without a loving nurse, searching for his need to be supplied." (Sophocles, Phil. 701±705). The art of medicine was painful to those who practiced it while bringing great benefits to those who needed it. The Hippocratic author of the treatise on *Airs* poignantly stated that "the physician sees terrible sights, touches unpleasant things, and harvests sorrows that are peculiarly his own from the misfortunes of others." Not by coincidence this saying was often cited by Christian authors.

Physicians perceived themselves as equally vulnerable to suffering as their patients; a late antique proverb conveyed the common perception that those "who treat others are themselves teeming with countless wounds." The touch of the wounded healer was a token of empathy, a way of alleviating "social pain." In the late 4th century, a "tactile revolution" took place that removed taboos from polluting objects: dead and infected bodies were no longer avoided but embraced. Christians worshipped the putrefying flesh of Stylite saints, and touched their relics, buried the homeless poor in 'all-hospitable' graves, tended the near-dying victims of plague, and kissed the wounds of lepers. The democratization of empathy, the birth of a more wide-ranging inclusive sensitivity, led to the birth of the hospital, and the increased visibility of the marginalized in the historical sources. The rise of a new civic elite, the Christian bishops, who searched for relative autonomy from the central power, tax-immunities and novel ways of self-legitimation vis-à-vis heretics, and the heterodox was instrumental in the establishment of philanthropic institutions. Out of sincere interest, but also in view of attracting donations to the church, they brought at the forefront of the public's attention the plight of the poor.

Around 370, the outbreak of famine in Cappadocia, and the Gothic invasion exacerbated the already existing diseases, leprosy being the most salient among them, as it epitomized all possible disabilities: blindness, mutilation, lesions on the body, difficulty breathing and eating. In their homilies 'De Pauperibus amandis,' Gregory of Nazianzus and Gregory of Nyssa vituperated against the ostracism of lepers, and preached the removal of the stigma of untouchability from their bodies: "People ran away from them, being almost angered for sharing even the same air with them." They drove them away from springs and houses, as if they were polluted. But if angels do not abominate to come into contact with humans, "if the Lord of the angels put on the stinking flesh ... so that He could heal your infirmities by means of His own touch," the Cappadocian bishops reasoned, then every person ought to give a helping hand to the outcasts of Roman society. In the same way that humans do not abominate the sick parts of their organism, they should not abominate the lepers who were members of the body of the church. Lepra was not contagious; it was caused by humoral imbalance. Besides, everyone had seen people who had devoted themselves to the care of lepers dying in perfect health in deep old age.

Gregory of Nazianzus and Gregory of Nyssa tried to dispel popular fears of disease on theological, humanitarian and empirical grounds, buttressed by current medical theories about infection. The example of a suffering god who did not flinch from putting on the polluting human flesh, served as a model of humility and compassion. Further, Basil of Caesarea, brother of Gregory of Nyssa, who had committed himself to the care of the lepers without getting infected by the disease, proved that the prevailing prejudices had no foundation.

Around 372, Basil had established a "new city" consisting of hospices for strangers and a leprosarium where nurses and physicians tended the sick. The Cappadocian bishop, according to his friend Gregory of Nazianzus, "did not disdain to honor the sick with his lips ... he embraced them like brothers. To him belonged the diseased and the treatment of the wounds and the imitation of Christ, cleansing leprosy not with words but with deeds." Thus, loyal to the Hippocratic ideal, bishops appropriated the sufferings of others, providing for the first-time healthcare for the indigent..

From the late 4th century onwards, hospitals, orphanages, shelters for women who had given birth, old age houses, inns for the poor, places for the care of the blind, or the nurture of infants provided some level of medical care, primarily but not exclusively, in the urban centers of Syria, Mesopotamia, Asia Minor, Palestine, and Armenia. There is some evidence that during periods of famine and epidemics, the establishment of philanthropic institutions accelerated. In some regions, the level of health care was, in certain respects, superior to that provided in 21st-century American hospitals. According to a recent estimate, the analogy 1 bed per 83 persons, the average in the hospitals of early-7th-century Hermopolis Magna in Egypt, compares favorably to 1 bed per 73 persons, the average in the six medical institutions of New Haven, Connecticut, today.

In the Sampson xenon in Constantinople, founded by Justinian in the early 6th century, physicians performed hernia operations. In the 10th century, a surgical operation performed in the capital of Byzantium on Siamese twins was partially and briefly successful. Constructions that could host 70 patients, more or less, flanked the monasteries. In the early 12th century, in the imperial foundation of the Pantocrator, a "teacher taught the student doctors of the hospital the knowledge of medicine in a consistent and zealous manner." The doctors working there were not "allowed to go out of the city to tend any of the ruling class, even if they were important and related to the emperor." There were two doctors for the women's ward, accompanied by one female doctor, four female assistants, and two female orderlies. As it is detailed in the foundation act, apart from the hospital and the old-age house, a lepers' sanatorium was established outside the city where care and "consolation of every kind" was provided to the afflicted.

Hospitals, in their majority, provided elementary care. But care could save lives. During epidemics, the provision of food and drink by nurturing nurses and doctors, and the observance of the elementary rules of hygiene may cause a dramatic fall in mortality rates.

In the latter half of the 6th century, an anonymous pilgrim to Palestine described a healing place for lepers at the hot springs of Elijah in Gadara. There they would be offered a free dinner at the nearby inn, and then they would sleep and dream of their cure near the water.

Thus, a community of untouchables was formed entitled to dreams of healing.

4. A Tactile Revolution for Today

In 2019, there were 700 colonies of lepers in India. The afflicted were allowed to interact only among themselves. Poor sanitary and socio-economic conditions account for the 100,000 new cases of leprosy each year. The current pandemic has reminded us of an "intersectional untouchability" consisting of the interlacing of social, sanitary, and psychological untouchability. The poor, and especially ethnic minorities, within the so-called developed world and the ever-emerging, ever-stagnating developing countries are the most vulnerable to disease and "social pain," as on many levels they have been bearing the brunt of discriminatory neoliberal policies. They have restricted access to vaccination but even when it is available, they are more likely to express vaccine hesitancy, especially those who have limited educational opportunities.

Accordingly, experts consider the leveling out of social inequalities as a necessary precondition for the containment of infectious diseases. On this account, a switch from a "profit economy" for the 1% to a "care economy" for the many appears all the more imperative. "Prosperity without growth" has to be pursued as envisioned by Tim Jackson: "Delivering the human services that improve the quality of our lives: nutrition, shelter, health, social care, education, leisure, recreation, and the maintenance and protection of physical and natural assets." Above all, time has to be liberated from the condition of artificial scarcity imposed on employees, chained in their wires. A tactile revolution for today's needs would be a reworking and democratizing of ancient medical ethics, so as to create a care economy that would sustain life and the planet. A health-care politics that would address the deleterious impact of "social pain" would be part of a revolutionary reorientation of existential priorities.

Medical anthropologist Arthur Kleinman described from personal experience the difficulties of being human: "Caregiving is not easy. It consumes time, energy, and financial resources. It sucks out strength and determination. It turns simple ideas of efficacy and hope into big question marks. It can amplify anguish and desperation. It can divide the self. It can bring out family conflicts."

Kleinman tended his wife Joan, his companion in life and work, when at the age of fifty-nine she developed a severe form of Alzheimer's disease. As he writes: "If the ancient Chinese perception is right that we are not born fully human, but only become so as we cultivate ourselves and our relations with others, then caregiving is one of those relationships and practices of self-cultivation that make us, even as we experience our limits and failures, more human."

In Ocean Vuong's novel *On Earth We're Briefly Gorgeous*, a heterotopia of care as service is being painted in a succinct ironic interlude to the violence inflicted on the protagonist during his childhood in Vietnam: "It's true that in Vietnamese we rarely say 'I love you,' and when we do, it is almost always in English. Care and love for us are pronounced clearest through service: plucking white hairs, pressing yourself on your son to absorb a plane's turbulence and, therefore, his fear. Or now as Lan called to me 'Little Dog get over here and help me help your mother.' And we knelt on each side of you, rolling out the hardened chords in your upper arms, then down to your wrists, your fingers. For a moment almost too brief to matter, this made sense—that three people on the floor, connected to each other by touch, made something like the word family."

Care as assistance to the more vulnerable is exemplified in the society of whales which spend hours together touching one another, exchanging caresses, to quote the scientific term, and shouldering the burden of the injured members of the family. Possibly whales constitute the most apposite model for today's tactile revolution.

Antigone Samellas is a historian living in Athens. Her research explores existential and contemporary issues in view of tracing the archaeology of moods and emotions.

Classen, Constance. The Deepest Sense: A Cultural History of Touch. Illinois: Illinois University Press, 2012.

Bakalar, Nicholas. "Are Robotic Surgeries Really Better?" The New York Times, August 16, 2021. Accessed October 15, 2021.

"'Hands of Love': Warm Latex Gloves Mimic Human Touch for COVID-19 Patients in Brazil." Reuters, April 20, 2021. https://www.reuters.com/world/americas/hands-love-warm-latex-gloves-mimic-human-touch-covid-19-patients-brazil-2021-04-20. Accessed October 15, 2021.

Moran, Joe. "The Power of Touch: Is This the Sense We Missed Most?" The Guardian, February 28, 2021. Accessed October 15, 2021.

Bishop, Claire. Artificial Hells: Participatory Art and the Politics of Spectatorship. London: Verso, 2012.

Jonze, Spike, director. Her. Annapurna Pictures, 2013.

Lingis, Alphonso. "In Touch." In Violence and Splendor, 81–4. Evanston: Northwestern University Press, 2011.

Eisenberger, Naomi. "The Neural Bases of Social Pain: Evidence for Shared Representations with Physical Pain." Psychosomatic Medicine 74, no. 2 (2012): 126–35.

Most, Glenn. Doubting Thomas. Cambridge MA: Harvard University Press, 2006.

Kuriguyama, Shigehisa. The Expressiveness of the Body and the Divergence of Greek and Chinese Medicine. New York: Zone Books, 2012.

Aristotle. Problems, edited and translated by Robert Mayhew. Cambridge MA: Harvard University Press, 2011.

Gregory of Nyssa. "On the Soul and Resurrection." In Gregorio di Nissa. Sull'Anima e la Resurrezione, edited by Ilaria Ramelli. Milan: Bompiani, 2007.

Lewis, Orly. "Marcellinus' De pulsibus: a Neglected Treatise on the Ancient 'Art of the Pulse.'" In Scripta Classica Israelica 36 (2015): 195–214.

Lewis, Orly. "The Practical Application of Ancient Pulse-Lore and Its Influence on the Patient-Doctor Interaction." In Homo Patiens – Approaches to the Patient in the Ancient World, edited by Georgia Petridou and Chiara Thumiger, 345–64. Leiden: Brill, 2016.

Kosak, Jennifer. "Therapeutic Touch and Sophocles' Philoctetes." Harvard Studies in Classical Philology 99 (1999): 93–134.

Sophocles. Philoctetes, edited and translated by Hugh Lloyd-Jones. Loeb Classical Library 21. Cambridge MA: Harvard University Press, 1994.

Plutarch. De Curiositate, edited and translated by Jean Durmontier. Paris: Budé, 1975.

Rose, George. "Do Not Fear the Smear: How to Overcome Anxiety about Cervical Screening," The Guardian, March 18, 2019. Accessed October 15, 2021.

Ivanova, Anna and Ingela Lundin Kvalem. "Psychological Predictors of Intention and Avoidance of Attending Organized Mammography Screening in Norway: Applying the Extended Parallel Process Model." BCM Women's Health 67 (2021).

Lacan, Jacques. "La Troisième. VIIème Congrès de l'école freudienne de Paris," translated by Yolande Szcech. https://www.academia.edu. Accessed April 7, 2021.

Hippocrate, Épidémies V et VII, edited and translated by Jacques Jouanna. Paris: Budé, 2011.

Thumiger, Chiara. A History of the Mind and Mental Health in Classical Greek Medical Thought. Cambridge: Cambridge University Press, 2017.

Downie, Robin. "Paying Attention: Hippocratic and Asklepian Approaches." Advances in Psychiatric Treatment 18, no. 5 (2012): 363–68.

Bernabò, Massimo, ed. La Collezione di Testi Chirurgici di Niceta: Firenze, plut. 74.7. Rome: Edizioni di Storia e Letteratura, 2010.

Clarke Kosak, Jennifer. "Interpretations of the Healer's Touch in the Hippocratic Corpus." In Homo Patiens – Approaches to the Patient in the Ancient World, edited by Georgia Petridou and Chiara Thumige, 247–64. Leiden: Brill, 2016.

Owen, Ron. Solon of Athens: Poet, Philosopher, Soldier, Statesman. Portland: Sussex Academic Press, 2010.

Petridou, Georgia. "Healing Shrines." In A Companion to Greek Science, Technology and Medicine, edited by Georgia L. Irby. London: Wiley-Blackwell, 2019.

Samellas, Antigone. Death in the Eastern Mediterranean. The Christianization of the East: An interpretation. Tübingen: Mohr Siebeck, 2002.

Gregory of Nazianzus, Oration 14 and 43. In Gregorio di Nazianzo, Tutte le Orazioni, edited by Claudio Moreschini. Milan: Bompiani, 2000.

Gregory of Nyssa. "De Pauperibus Amandis." In Grégoire de Nysse, Six homélies pastorales, edited and translated by Pierre Maraval, SC 588. Paris: Cerf, 2017.

Anderson, Mark. "Hospitals, Hospices and Shelters for the Poor in Late Antiquity." PhD diss., Yale, 2012.

Thomas, John and Angela Constantinides Hero, eds. Byzantine Monastic Foundation Documents. A Complete Translation of the Surviving Founders' Typika and Testaments. Vol. 2. Washington: Dumbarton Oaks, 2000.

Miller, Timothy S., and John W. Nesbitt. Walking Corpses. Leprosy in Byzantium and the Medieval West. Ithaca: Cornell University Press, 2014.

Renberg, Gil H. Where Dreams May Come. Incubation Sanctuaries in the Greco-Roman World. Vol. 2. Leiden, Boston: Brill, 2017.

Mandavilli, Apoorva. "In India a Renewed Fight Against Leprosy." The New York Times, April 17, 2019. Accessed October 15, 2021.

Pescari Moreira, Julia Agostino Strina, Joilda Silva Nery, Lacita Menezes Skalinski, Kaio Vinicius Freitas de Andrade, Maria Lucia F. Penna, Elizabeth B. Brickley, Laura C. Rodrigues, Mauricio Lima Barreto, and Gerson Oliveira Penna. "Socioeconomic Risk Markers of Leprosy in High-burden Countries: A Systematical Review and Meta-analysis." PLOS. Neglected Tropical Diseases, July 9, 2018: 1–20.

Gayer-Anderson, Charlotte, et al. "Impacts of Social Isolation among Disadvantaged and Vulnerable Groups during Public Health Crises." ESRC, Centre For Society and Mental Health. Kings College, June 2020. https://esrc.ukri.org/news-events-and-publications/evidence-briefings/impacts-of-social-isolation-among-disadvantaged-and-vulnerable-groups-during-public-health-crises. Accessed October 15, 2021.

Jackson, Tim. Prosperity without Growth. Foundations for the Economy of Tomorrow, second edition. London: Routledge, 2017.

Kleinman, Arthur. "Catastrophe and Caregiving: The Failure of Medicine as an Art." The Lancet 371, no. 9606 (2008): 22–23.

Kleinman, Arthur. "The Art of Medicine. Caregiving: The Odyssey of Becoming More Human." The Lancet 373, no. 9660 (2009): 292–93.

Vuong, Ocean. On Earth We're Briefly Gorgeous. New York: Penguin, 2019.

Christakis, Nicholas A. Blueprint – The Evolutionary Origins of a Good Society. New York: Little Brown, Spark, 2019.

In the shadows of its interior, seven men are asleep. The rock encases and shelters them. They wear loose robes of grey, red, blue, tawny brown, purple. They lie close together. Some are barefoot, some are shod. There is a brotherliness to their pose—a tenderness to the way one of the sleepers rests his hand on the brow of another. These are the seven sleepers of Ephesus, known in Arabic as 'ashab al kahf', the 'people of the cave', and theirs is a story of waiting in darkness, within rock, until it is safe to emerge. Their story recurs in the Christian and Islamic traditions; it is there in the Qur'an, in the Roman Martyrology. The young men, fleeing religious persecution in the city of Ephesus, enter a cave mouth that leads them deep into the mountain. In that den of night, exhausted by flight, they lie down and sleep, they will sleep for 300 years—and when they emerge all danger will be gone.

> — Robert Macfarlane, *Underland: A Deep Time Journey*, London: Penguin Books, 2020.

My Grandmother's Desire to Heal: A Pilgrimage to Lesbos
Valentina Karga

As most of the Greeks I know, I grew up with a religious grandmother. She would light the oil lamp in the typical station many Greek Orthodox households have with paintings of Panagia (Mother Mary), saints Raphael, Nicholas and Irini, Jesus on the cross, and Saint George who kills the Dragon.

Grandmother searched for healing through blind faith in God, as it was taught to her by her family and schooling. She felt especially connected to Saint Raphael. She had been calling him every night to cure her in her sleep. Saint Raphael, martyred in Lesbos in 1463, is known for performing healing miracles, about which my grandmother would eagerly read in the monastery's leaflets. In this text, I am trying to understand what she was seeking to heal from in a speculative and forensic way—as she didn't have an apparent health issue. Why was she looking for a miracle? What is the unspoken truth of who my grandmother really was, a complex truth I was too young to understand?

I only remember her being often uncomfortable with bloating and constipation. As a child, I found it always a bit far-fetched to need a miracle to be healed from toilet-related problems. What did grandma want to heal from? After long research, I finally arrived at trauma-informed therapy and polyvagal theory. Through this, I understood how many digestion and gut-related issues are intertwined with mental health. Moreover, the more I understood mental health, the more I can see how earlier theories and practices of medicine that did not understand trauma from a nervous system approach and the gut-brain connection, or the body-mind connection; also, did not acknowledge the suppression of women in a patriarchal regime. This left people like my grandmother even more traumatized, lonely, and unhealed.

Contemporary polyvagal theory[1] explains that trauma is whatever pushes the activation of the nervous system beyond its ability to self-regulate. When a stressful experience pushes the system beyond its limits, it can become stuck in agitation. A nervous system is agitated when it is on fight, flight or freeze response and relaxed when it is on 'rest and digest.' When a system is overstimulated and agitated for a long time, we can experience anxiety, panic, anger, hyperactivity, and restlessness. The nervous system can get agitated by a one-time dramatic event and by long-term exposure to low-stress conditions. "A range of psychiatric disorders such as anxiety, depression, and post-traumatic stress disorder frequently co-occur with functional gastrointestinal disorders. The risk of these pathologies is particularly high in those with a history of trauma, abuse, and chronic stress."[2]

My grandfather returned from the Greek Civil War in 1949 with post-traumatic stress disorder, which back then, in 1950s rural Greece, didn't even have, let alone a context to cure it. Apart from having had to kill others to survive, he also had to endure the loss of his beloved female partner, with whom he was fighting together in the partisan party. She got shot in his arms. Developing intimacy while fighting a war, learning to love and kill simultaneously; what a paradoxical psychological state to be trapped in. His unresolved trauma led him into anger which was manifested as domestic violence, primarily towards my grandmother, whom he married a couple of years after the war, and sometimes also towards my mother when she was a child. Chronically exposed to domestic violence, which takes a toll on the nervous system, my grandmother developed gut imbalances, anxiety, and mood disorders. Today, these are all proof of a dysregulated nervous system that suffered trauma, but, at that time, her trauma was not acknowledged as one, and there was no guidance for such healing. Undereducated women like her, and later even my mother, in rural Greece, for up until the 1980s or even the 1990s, were led to neglect their traumas, gaslighted[3] from centuries of male oppression. Moreover, they were ashamed to discuss it among other women in their communities, who probably suffered the same. Thus, they only had the church, praying and sleeping, as their means of self-help to counterbalance the lack of therapy and information available. Grandmother has always been a great sleeper, my mom recollects. Even in periods of intense worry and distress, she could sleep well. My mother, having suffered from insomnia and experienced its terrible effects on mood and mental health, believes that my grandmother's ability to sleep well was what kept her sane and supported her faith in healing.

To elaborate on my grandparents' complex reality, I want to draw some insights from bell hooks and her book *All About Love*, which outlines how men are led to invest in a false sense of masculine identity that masks or suppresses true feelings. "Estrangement from feelings makes it easier for men to lie because they are often in a trance state, utilizing survival strategies of asserting manhood they learned as boys. This inability to connect with others carries with it an inability to assume responsibility for causing pain." She continues elaborating how "psychologically and/or physically abused children have been taught by parenting adults that abuse can co-exist with love." And how they end up repeating the same patterns of abuse and care in their own dysfunctional relationships; often, even in an adult stage, they choose to remain in these relationships by "denying the abuse and focusing on the random acts of care."[4]

What did grandma want to heal from? I can only assume that apart from the war, both my grandparents have inherited a history of lovelessness from their families. Although Christian religion is based on love, preaching in Christian churches—whose influence on many Greek families was significant—often ignored gender equalities. These views were shaped by the Greek philosophical tradition, notably Aristotle, who "believed that women lacked autonomous reason, and were therefore inherently inferior and dependent on the male."[5] In many of the New Testament doctrines, it is underlined that woman was made from man, thus coming second in nature, but first in sin, since she was the one first convinced to eat the apple. According to bell hooks, love and domination cannot coexist. However, my grandmother forgave my grandfather and continuously cared for him until the moment she died. I don't know if she had a choice, since everything in her upbringing probably led to a belief that women had to serve their husbands and that good Christians had to endure suffering. On the other hand, it was as if she could see beyond his anger his own suffering and that my grandfather too, was therefore a victim of patriarchal masculinity.

With an agitated nervous system and no understanding of what sort of severe trauma she was in, she believed that she was the problem. Trying to heal in a culture so dismissive of emotional wounds, women and all those who dared express them were made to feel 'crazy' for having all those emotions. To deal with this burden, she turned to God. And I believe that through this, she at least became aware of the feelings she was yearning for: love, safety, care, healing; values that stand out in the Christian religion. However, she never dared to question the contradictions within this religion regarding women's place in society. What strikes me is that she never gave up on her belief in healing. She persisted on a pilgrimage to the Monastery of Saint Raphael on Lesbos island, where she hoped to finally find cure during her sleep.

    Grandmother eventually made the trip in the early 1990s and came back exhilarated. She had not traveled much and only knew bits of northern Greece. Because she didn't have a concrete plan for this trip, she opted for the 7-day all-inclusive package. A bus picked her up from Aghios Nikolaos, our village in Chalkidiki, and brought her and other pilgrims from the region to the port of Kavala where they took an 18-hour ferry. Upon arrival in Lesbos, the bus took them straight to Saint Raphael's monastery, a female convent, where they slept in the monastery's dormitories for visitors. She told me about the numerous quests for healing she heard from the other pilgrims, meaning that she encountered others like her, believers in healing, and that must have been an affirming experience. Every day the bus would pick them up and bring them to see more churches and monasteries on Lesbos. She

Fig. 18
Monastery of Saint Raphael, Karyes hill,
Lesbos, digital drawing, 2021.

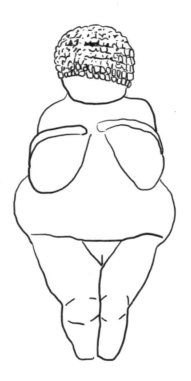

Fig. 19
Venus of Willendorf,
digital drawing, 2021.

made temporary friends on that trip, opening up in sharing her story, just like others shared their stories with her. Several studies have proven the adverse effects on physical and mental health when people withhold emotions. Instead, "when disclosing deeply personal experiences, there are immediate changes in brain-wave patterns, skin conductance levels, and overt behavioral correlates of the letting-go experience. After confessions, significant drops in blood pressure and heart rate and improvements in immune function occur. In the weeks and months afterward, people's physical and psychological health improves."[6] Moreover, going on a pilgrimage and the prospect of healing offers people a way out of hopelessness and despair. The positive emotions associated with the trip, the preparation, the anticipation, seeing new places, and meeting new people could have strengthened her immune system and assisted in the body's natural capacity to heal.

While my grandfather had many stories from the war to tell, my grandmother was only telling me the same story, about her trip to Lesbos island: about the monastery's beautiful location, its lovely flower garden, and the nuns' soothing singing. She also told me about the inspiring Mother Superior Eugenia Klidara, a well-educated and well-traveled woman and published author who created this monastery. The story of that woman reminded me that even throughout Christianity, and especially in its early times, there have been women inspired by Christian ideals and became founders of monasteries, pilgrimage leaders, pioneers of education, hermits, caretakers of the poor and sick. In fact, it was a woman who invented the first kind of a modern hospital.[7] I believe that, in a way, the institution of Church was to my grandmother similar to what art is for me. Knowing more about all these pioneer women, like Eugenia Klidara, must have been for her as inspiring and empowering is for me to meet pioneer female artists and writers. However, while growing up I could sense that there was a feminine disempowerment put in place by religion, although I did not know yet how to point it out. In highschool, I was terrified reading about the torture of philosopher Hypatia, someone I looked up to, being brutally murdered by a mob of Christians in 415. Hypatia's murder was a landmark in the course of history in regards to knowledge praticed by women, whether that was healing, philisophy or mathematics. After that event, women interested in knowledge would be condemned as heretics and witches. Therefore they kept these practices a secret. Apart from the mind, I also find interesting what happened to the body of women. In the countless prehistoric figurines, such as the Venus of Willendorf, the female archetype is nude, lusty, voluptuous, with exaggerated sexual features. She clearly gives birth through this body, and this is something to celebrate, not to be ashamed of. The Christian era, with Panagia as the new model of a woman, changed this course radically. I always found her to be a tragic, dramatic figure, because she is mostly remembered as a devastated mother, whose child died, and most of the time I felt compassion for her. But, all the other aspects of her actions and personality are not as widely known. In my teenage years, her story of having given birth without sexual intercourse, sounded to me more of a lie than a miracle. I was angry that sex had such an infamous role in Christian Greece and that the feminine role model was that of a mourning mother disconnected from her senses and body. This model of Panagia created a culture of shame, and disconnection from sexuality. While during my childhood, I was happy to see more and more women focusing on their careers or engaging in intellectual professions, women's connection to their bodies was still a taboo. I avoided discussing this fundamental change in my beliefs with my grandmother because it only confused and upset her.

As I was growing up I was trying to trace connections in the succession of the Earth Mother by Panagia, and in the succession of religions, when looking at their different aspects. Some of these successions sometimes take material forms, as in the case of stones and marbles taken from ancient pagan temples and reused in the construction of Christian churches built on top of them. I can recall my bewilderment when taught about these processes while studying architecture, and therefore, recalling my grandmother's story from Lesbos, I wanted to find out more about the architectural history of Saint Raphael's monastery in Lesbos and its surroundings. What I found is that the chapel of Aghia Paraskevi, where Christian priests are buried and pilgrims go to pay homage to their remnants, is built on top of an ancient sanctuary initially dedicated to Artemis, and later replaced by another, dedicated to Asklepios. Also, in 1986, archaeologists Caroline and Hector Williams excavated a sanctuary dedicated to Demeter and Kore, that was an important site for the female-only nocturnal festival Thesmophoria, which was held not too far from the monastery. They believe that this sanctuary was built on top of an even earlier one, dedicated to the prehistoric Earth Mother, as they found a large clay roof tile with the word "MATROON" engraved onto it; the word probably means "sanctuary of the Mother Goddess."[8]

When I read Audre Lorde's *The Power of the Erotic* as an adult, it resonated with me that part of my grandmother's trauma was a severe cut from her female power, what Lorde names as the "erotic" which reminds me of Panagia's representation. "The erotic is a resource within each of us that lies in a deeply female and spiritual plane, firmly rooted in the power of our unexpressed or unrecognized feeling. [...] When I speak of the erotic, then, I speak of it as an assertion of the life force of women; of that creative energy empowered, the knowledge and use of which we are now reclaiming in our language, our history, our dancing, our loving, our work, our lives.

Fig. 20
Chapel in a rock, Aghia Paraskevi, on the hill above the settlement with the same name, Lesbos, digital drawing, 2021.

[...] we have attempted to separate the spiritual and the erotic, thereby reducing the spiritual to a world of flattened affect, a world of the ascetic who aspires to feel nothing. But nothing is farther from the truth. For the ascetic position is one of the highest fears… The erotic is the nurturer or nursemaid of all our deepest knowledge."[9]

I don't remember Grandmother's pilgrimage because I was very young, but my mom recalls it as a transition from her being overly anxious, unhappy, and constantly worried, to gradually—within one or two years—someone who had found at least some inner peace, as she was looking more relaxed. However, neither my mom and grandfather nor I can recall my grandmother mentioning any meeting with Saint Raphael in her sleep. I don't think my grandmother found this miraculous healing in the way she was looking for. Nevertheless, a mysterious fact was added to her life, which everyone in the family confirms: her regular dream encounters with Panagia. This sole mysterious element in my grandmother's 'nightlife' is what drives me to believe that something more complex must have happened during her visit to Lesbos.

Today, recalling the fragments of her memories and the stories she told me, merged with the stories that moved me since I was a kid, I realized that there was a continuous feminine presence in them, and I somehow like to imagine my grandmother unconsciously sensing it too. In her absence, I attempt to understand her need and desire to heal, or the kind of healing she was hoping for. I can only look at the different pieces of this puzzle. The Temple to which the sanctuary of Demeter and Kore was connected to, was never found to this date. Can it be that it is under the monastery's accommodation where my grandmother slept? Or maybe that she also visited the chapel of Aghia Paraskevi that earlier was the location of the Asklepios healing cult? That is very likely since she was on religious sightseeing. Or, maybe, part of Mother Superior Eugenia Klidara's intentions in creating this place was to maintain the healing processes long-ago present in the area? Or, my grandmother's experience of sharing her unspoken emotions with people who understood, or at least listened to her, lifted enough of her burden and made her feel physically better. I don't know. What I know is that grandmother believed in healing so wholeheartedly, as if there was an invisible string connecting possibly all female ancestors that were connected to their "erotic powers" that could never be entirely cut off, despite all the gaslighting from centuries of patriarchal oppression. She, and all the women of her generation who went through similar experiences, did not fully manage to become aware of this connection during their lifetimes. Healing is finding the way back to yourself, and, I believe, is happening in stages. Some stages are unconscious, so perhaps, this is what my grandmother achieved, and others need one's awareness and understanding of what really happened.

Rest in peace, Grandmother. I carry on with our healing.

Valentina Karga is an artist living in Berlin with a background in architecture. She teaches art and design in Hamburg.

1. Polyvagal theory was introduced in 1994 by Stephen Porges, director of the Brain-Body Center at the University of Illinois at Chicago. Stephen W. Porges, The Polyvagal Theory: Neurophysiological Foundations of Emotions, Attachment, Communication, and Self-regulation (New York: W. W. Norton & Company, 2011).

2. Jacek Kolacz, Katja K. Kovacic and Stephen W. Porges, "Traumatic Stress and the Autonomic Brain-gut Connection in Development: Polyvagal Theory as an Integrative Framework for Psychosocial and Gastrointestinal Pathology," Developmental Psychobiology 61, no. 5 (2019): 796–809.

3. Gaslighting is a colloquialism for a specific type of manipulation where the manipulator is successful in having the target (a person or a group of people) question their own reality, memory or perceptions. There is often a power dynamic in gaslighting where the target is vulnerable because they are fearful of losses associated with challenging the manipulator. Gaslighting is not necessarily malicious or intentional, although in some cases it is. APA Dictionary of Psychology. https://dictionary.apa.org, accessed July 7, 2021

4. bell hooks, All About Love: New Visions (New York: William Morrow, 2000), 25.

5. Rosemary Radford Ruether, "Sexism and Misogyny in the Christian Tradition: Liberating Alternatives," Buddhist-Christian Studies 34 (2014): 83–94, accessed July 13, 2021.

6. Robert A. Scott, Miracle Cures: Saints, Pilgrimage, and the Healing Powers of Belief, 1st ed. (Berkeley, CA: University of California Press, 2010), 56.

7. Mary Kenny, "Patriarchy and Christian Feminism," Studies: An Irish Quarterly Review 95, no. 378 (Summer 2006): 175–81, accessed July 13, 2021.

8. "Also, known as Cybelle or the Great Mother, she is a pre-Greek fertility deity of Asia-Minor whose worship became increasingly important in the Greek and later, Roman world." Hector Williams, "Secret Rites of Lesbos," Archaeology 47, no. 4 (1994): 35–40.

9. Audre Lorde, Sister Outsider: Essays and Speeches (New York: Ten Speed Press, 1984).

Image credits

Fig. 1, 4-6, 9-10
Vasilis Voskós

Fig. 2
Antigone Samellas

Fig. 3
Dimitra Kondylatou

Fig. 7-8
Dimitrios Bosnakis

Fig. 11
American School of Classical Studies at Athens, Corinth Excavations

Fig. 12
Markela Bgiala

Fig. 13, 17
Bayerische Staatsbibliothek München, Cod. lat. 14300

Fig. 14
Codex Nicetas Plut. 74, f. 185v

Fig. 15-16
Codex Nicetas Plut. 74.7, f. 197r

Fig. 18-20
Valentina Karga

every effort has been made to trace copyright holders and obtain their permission to use copyright material. kyklàda.press apologizes for any errors or omissions in this list and would be grateful if notified of any corrections that should be incorporated in future reprints of this book.

Colophon

published in 2021 by
kyklàda.press

contributors
David Bergé
Milica Ilić
Antigone Samellas
Valentina Karga

copy editing
and proofreading
EG (Geli Mademli,
Eleanna Papathanasiadi)

managing editor
Dimitra Kondylatou

thanks to
Robert Macfarlane
Ilan Manouach
Silke Neumann
Tassos Papaioannou
Anna Protopapadaki
Jan Ritsema

design
Costas Kalogeropoulos
with Roland Brauchli
and David Bergé

distribution
Books People Places
and kyklàda.press

series direction
David Bergé

kyklàda.press co-founders
Juan Duque
Dimitra Kondylatou
Nicolas Lakiotakis

kyklàda.press team 2021
Juan Duque
Milica Ilić
Dimitra Kondylatou
Nicolas Lakiotakis
Antigone Samellas

kyklàda.press
is an imprint of
PHOTOGRAPHIC
EXPANDED
PUBLISHING
ATHENS

Free Love Paid Love (2020)
Expressions of Affection in Mykonos

Nowhere in Cycladic culture has love been defined in a singular all-encompassing manner. Forces of attraction, affection, connection, and relation were ascribed in a plurality of ways. Through symposia in Delos, the tax haven of antiquity, 17th-century transactions of love involving pirates, slaves, and Mykonians; naturist communities reliving sexual freedom in the 1960-70s and 21st-century tourists quest in search of love, free or paid; this book gathers fragments of expressions of affection across Mykonos island. Mykonos has long defined itself as a self-ruling place far away from realities lived elsewhere.

The Architect is Absent (2020)
Approaching the Cycladic Holiday House

The white cubical house, the vernacular architecture in the Aegean Archipelago, knows no author. Its capacity to resist harsh climatic and topographic circumstances has been improved and adjusted through time and seems today close to perfection. The white-washed Cycladic House has become iconic to the image of Greece through the construction of national and tourism narratives. What happens when an architect steps into this process of anonymous transmission of skills? In 1966 music composer, architect, and engineer Iannis Xenakis articulated a response to this tradition and designed, from his base in Paris, a holiday house on the island of Amorgos while choosing to remain absent throughout the construction process.

Public Health in Crisis (2020)
Confined in the Aegean Archipelago

Epidemics and pandemics undermine societies and highlight the vulnerability of relations people have created to the land, other species, and each other. This book presents fragments of disease management in the Mediterranean from the 15th century onwards and in the Aegean Archipelago in the last two centuries. From religious to medical approaches to the Bubonic Plague, through the creation of lazarettos, to the famine in occupied Syros, to ghost ships drifting on the Mediterranean: citizens are forced to avoid citizens. Public health in crisis: confinement versus mobility, awakening memories of totalitarian regimes.

The Sleeping Hermaphrodite (2020)
Waking up from a Lethargic Confinement

What can a reclining marble sculpture, conceived through a myth in Greek antiquity, tell us today about the fluidity of our gender construction? What has been the role of aesthetic and historical canons in the construction of the female and male genders? Is 'the sleeping Hermaphrodite' really asleep? Or has she/he been induced to a long lethargic state, punished and confined by the history of gender normalization?

kyklàda.press titles

Architectures of Healing (2021)
Cure through Sleep, Touch, and Travel

Today, many feel fettered by insomnia, untouchability, and restrictions on movement. Looking for a more holistic approach to bodily and mental health, this book explores architectures and elementary forms of care and healing in different time periods: from the powers of sleep, touch, and travel in Asklepieia, the ancient healing temples for divine dream encounters alleviating the pain of the ailing pilgrim; to the attentiveness carried through the healing touch from the establishment of Byzantine hospitals till our times; to a pilgrimage center in modern-day Lesbos on a personal search for healing from the traumas of war and patriarchy; to the liberating and self-preserving powers of sleep as a healing response to past and current systems of oppression.

(Forced) Movement (2021)
Across the Aegean Archipelago

What would be of contemporary culture if we did not recognize the impact of migration in cultural and socio-economic crossings? This book explores human migration in different times, contexts, and geographies surrounding the Aegean Sea. Through an assemblage of voices, lived experiences, historical documents, urban and rural dislocations, this publication examines responses to mobility of the ones on the move, and of the ones living in the destinations the former are heading to. It speaks of the sacrifices one is forced to make en route and at its antipode; the implications of voluntary migration to a place, steered by investment in real estate.

KY
KLÀ
DA

Dry heat on your body. Bronze grasses and rocks, cactae, aloe vera. Concrete, asphalt, and marble, the Cycladic Landscape is both rural and urban: the Aegean Archipelago, south-east of Athens, extends into the city hills.

    Through navigation, the Westernized sense of perspective has established a common horizon, simplifying islands as visual spots at the surface of the sea. Islands are not exotic entities isolated in the sea waters. Islands remain interconnected with the mainland and each other, from the top of the mountains to the hidden topographies of the seabed: a myriad of creatures and non-organic matter which lives in constant symbiosis with water; tectonic plates, fossil fuel pipes, and data cables.

    kyklàda.press is a small imprint, producing a series of texts resonating with phenomena in the Aegean Archipelago. kyklàda.press is a not-for-profit book project driven by a transdisciplinary team directed by David Bergé, exploring critical and experimental positions in writing. With each volume in this series, we are slowly forming a catalogue of liquid forms of modernity: corporeal bodies—historical and actual, real, and imaginative.